NALA THE HERO HUSKY

Written by:
Morgan Hritz

Illustrated by:
James Crumby

Copyright © 2021 Morgan Hritz
All rights reserved
First Edition

Fulton Books, Inc.
Meadville, PA

Published by Fulton Books 2021

ISBN 978-1-63860-308-5 (paperback)
ISBN 978-1-63860-310-8 (hardcover)
ISBN 978-1-63860-309-2 (digital)

Printed in the United States of America

Dedication

Thank you to my family and friends who have always been there to support my dreams no matter how bad the anxiety got. Y'all are the real heroes. And of course, thank you to Nala (and Zazu) who are truly the best dogs a girl could ask for.

When anxiety was great within, your consolation brought me joy.
—Psalm 94:19

Anxiety weighs down the heart, but a kind word cheers it up.
—Proverbs 12:25

Nala is a Siberian husky. Her owner, Miss Hritz, got her when she was only eight weeks old! They have been best friends since day one.

Nala and Miss Hritz do everything together. Some of their favorites are biking, hiking, kayaking, and running.

Ever since Miss Hritz became a teacher, she had wanted a dog to be a part of her classroom. Nala was just the dog to make her dream a reality.

Nala is a special dog. When she was only a few months old, she started training.

When she was six months old, she finished her basic training and became an emotional support animal.

An emotional support animal is any animal that makes you feel safe and comfortable. That definitely describes Nala.

When Nala was one year old, she graduated training and became an official therapy dog.

To become a therapy dog, Nala had to pass a test. It was a test that she had worked really hard to do well on.

Now that Nala was officially a therapy dog, she could go to school with Miss Hritz!

Nala loved school! She loved hanging out with all her friends in Miss Hritz's classroom.

Nala was amazing and super helpful. When teachers or students were having a tough day, they would hang out with Nala for a while.

People would come to see Nala when they had small problems and big problems!

When anyone felt like screaming or crying, Nala would rush to their side. No matter how tired she was, Nala was right there to help.

Nala even helped with injuries. She was there for people who had a papercut, seizures, or a nasty stomach bug.

No matter what the issue was, Nala was there.

This is how Nala gained the name "Nala the Hero Husky" because Nala saves the world, one person at a time.

Back when Miss Hritz was in high school, she had many health problems. Eventually, she was told she had anxiety.

Anxiety is how your body deals with stress. It makes doing new things very difficult. Anxiety makes your body act in strange ways.

Anxiety can come out of your body in many different ways. Sometimes your heart beats really fast—you sweat, you shake, feel tired, feel dizzy, can't concentrate, can't sleep, get an upset stomach, and many, many other things. For Miss Hritz, she just wants to hide from everybody. Her heart starts beating fast and she can't catch her breath. It feels like no matter what she does, she will never be good enough.

When Miss Hritz got Nala, everything seemed to be easier. Her anxiety didn't come around as often.

It helped knowing that no matter what, Nala was there for Miss Hritz. No matter how many times Miss Hritz failed, no matter how many times Miss Hritz wanted to run and hide, no matter how many times Miss Hritz's anxiety came back, Nala would still love her.

Then something happened... Nala became nervous to go to school. She didn't want to be around people as much as she did before.

It started small. Nala would go home and hide under the bed or under a blanket or in the bathtub.

Then she started hiding from teachers at school. She even ran away from a few!

Miss Hritz didn't know what to do, so she took Nala to the vet.

The vet told Miss Hritz Nala had anxiety.

Miss Hritz was devastated. How was Nala supposed to help people at school if she was filled with so much anxiety and fears?

After many failures, Nala and Miss Hritz figured a few things out that helped ease their anxiety together.

Even though they don't have everything figured out, they are working through these struggles together.

One thing that seems to help is a great big bear hug from someone they love!

Sometimes Nala will curl up next to someone who makes her feel safe. A couple of times, she has even gotten in someone's lap to get a bear hug!

Something that helps Miss Hritz is music! Whether it is listening to music or singing and playing piano, the stress just seems to fade away.

Come to find out, this seems to help Nala as well! She crawls under the piano and listens to Miss Hritz play. This usually puts her right to sleep!

That's another thing that helps Nala cope with her anxiety. A good nap will usually ease her frantic thoughts!

When Nala is really sleeping, she sleeps in the strangest positions!

Nala and Miss Hritz also figured out that sometimes you just have to work through the anxiety.

In doing this, Nala has learned so many new things!

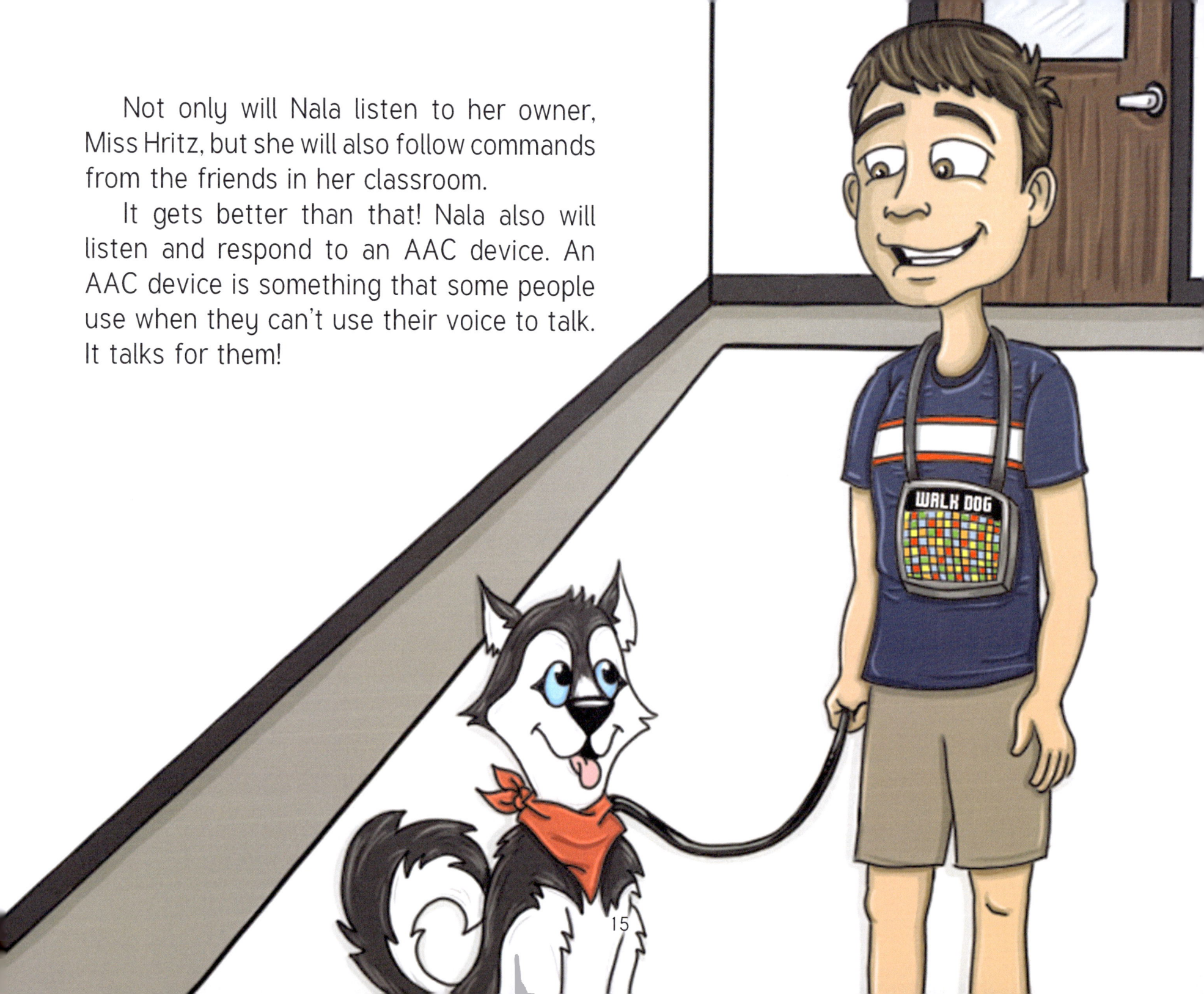

Not only will Nala listen to her owner, Miss Hritz, but she will also follow commands from the friends in her classroom.

It gets better than that! Nala also will listen and respond to an AAC device. An AAC device is something that some people use when they can't use their voice to talk. It talks for them!

That's not even it! A student in Miss Hritz's class taught Nala how to understand a bit of her language too! Nala knows a couple of words in American Sign Language. Her favorite is finding the hidden treat after she is given the sign for where.

Another fun thing that Nala has learned is how to talk! She uses buttons to tell Miss Hritz what she needs or wants. Her favorite buttons are Walk and Treat!

Sometimes working through your anxiety just isn't enough. In this case, Nala and Miss Hritz have learned it's okay to take a break.

Do something fun or get away for a while! You deserve it!

One of Miss Hritz and Nala's favorite ways to ease anxiety is to read.
Nala loves to curl up in someone's lap as they read her a good book.

If none of those work, Nala and Miss Hritz surround themselves with people that love them. Nala's world was turned upside down when Miss Hritz brought home another dog, Zazu. Zazu may cause Nala and Miss Hritz quite a bit of stress, but he also helps support them when they are feeling overwhelmed. Sometimes the things that cause us the most anxiety are the things that can also help ease it.

It is okay to be anxious. It happens to even the best people (and dogs).

When life seems to be moving way too fast and you are struggling to keep up, try one (or more) of Nala's tricks. And always remember, you are not a mistake. You are not invisible. You are not a burden. You are important. You are worth it. You are so much more than your anxiety. You are perfect.

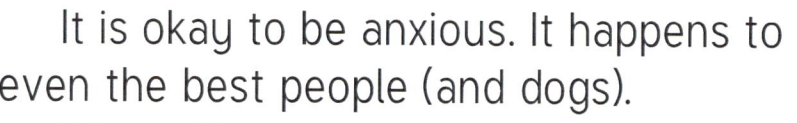

About the Author

    Morgan has been a special education teacher since 2016. She has a bachelor's degree in early childhood education, a master's degree in special education, and is currently working on her doctorate in educational leadership. In her free time, Morgan enjoys reading, crafting, playing piano, or exploring nature.

    Nala has been a registered emotional support animal since 2017. In 2019, Nala graduated with her therapy pet certification and began work at school the same year. When not at school, Nala can usually be found napping or outside with Morgan and Zazu.

    To follow Morgan, Nala, and Zazu on social media, go to Therapy Dog Nala and Zazu (@nala.and.zazu) on Facebook or Instagram.

www.ingramcontent.com/pod-product-compliance
Ingram Content Group UK Ltd.
Pitfield, Milton Keynes, MK11 3LW, UK
UKRC030205240426
12048UKWH00004B/89